My Teenage Brain
Ava Lafrance

Cosmic Teapot Publishing
Hanmer, ON

My Teenage Brain

Copyright © 2019 by Ava Lafrance

ISBN: 978-1-988762-15-9

Cover by Kiandra Holmes

Published by Cosmic Teapot Publishing
Hanmer, ON, Canada
www.cosmicteapot.net

Ordering Information:
Quantity sales. Special discounts are available on quantity purchases by corporations, associations, and others. For details, contact the publisher at the email address above.

Ava Lafrance is currently a student studying at Confederation Secondary School in Val Caron, Ontario. She is working towards her high school diploma. She is actively involved in many school activities like student parliament and football.

With a passion for poetry, she is excited about her first release, *My Teenage Brain*. She was inspired to write poetry from a class project that turned into something more important. This is the first of many poetry collections that she is excited to release to the world.

Thank you for reading!

Acknowledgments:

I'd like to thank everyone who has supported me throughout this process. Thank you for everything you have done. My mom and dad, you've supported me through everything and this is for you. I'd also like to thank my aunt Jennifer who has inspired me to share my poems by letting me share my poetry for the first time with her. You inspire me every day. As well as my friends Kiandra and Alex who seem to be able to help me through my creative blocks. Thank you to all my family and friends for always having my back on this. This one is dedicated to all my friends and family who love me unconditionally.

Table of Contents

Intro

i wonder
Why are we here?
Why are we born on this planet,
In this place?
Why do we live where we live?
Why do we do what we do?
Why are the people we know the people we know?
The teenage brain
Too many questions
It can cause a scene
Will we ever know our true place?
Perhaps if we make a stink
There will be a day where we find our missing link

A mellow place

My mind
A busy place
Full of aeroplanes and railway trains
A few changes have been made in my busy city called
brain
Many new things being analyzed and categorized
i try and try to make it a mellow place
i just can't finalize the change
i guess i like things busy up in my brain
Even though it's been making me feel kind of dizzy
i guess i need to learn to like my little city.

Curious or paranoid

We question everything and everyone
i assume it is because we are curious
But are we curious?
Or are we paranoid?
Paranoid; a state of mind we aren't willing to- face
It makes me think
Do we know more than we make ourselves believe?
Somewhere in the back of our brains
Hiding away so we won't let ourselves make a stink
Or then again we are probably just curious
i shouldn't say anything
i don't want to make anyone believe
Maybe we know more than we think

Monsters

There's this monster taking over you
It's down right controlling
It's taking over your thoughts
It's taking over your heart
It's taking over your soul

i pray one day you'll make it out okay
You are strong and brave
And the monsters inside
They do not define you

i pray again
That one day you realize
The monsters have no place inside of you
They do not define you

Fear

Humans.
Hear.
Fear.
The tip toes
And the sketchy hellos
Fear.
Something we shouldn't be able to hear
But we can
With every little sound
Humans.
Hear.
Fear.

Words

Words
Oh they say a lot
Ready to do damage in milliseconds
Do they create more damage than we know?
Sure does, don't you think so?

Butterflies

You make me have butterflies
And believe your perfect little lies

i try to escape your incredible smile
But you know maybe
Just maybe
i can wait a while

You, heart

i call upon my brain
To make my decisions
But you, heart come and get in the way
You chose love when you know i do not want it
You chose heartbreak instead of holding it all in
i just want my brain to tell me what to say
You, heart never seem to pick the right
pathway

A dumb thought that became a poem

i put up a wall
When you said you didn't feel the same way
Now that it has changed
i'll need some time and space
To figure out if the beauty of us still lies in our
presence
i do not know if i'll ever feel the same way again
Even though it was some sort of marvelous heaven
Please listen when i say
i love you
But i don't know if
i love you
will ever be the same

Jealous

Jealous of her
Being able to talk to you
Jealous of her
Being able to touch you
Jealous of her
Being able to help you
Jealous of her
Being able to love you

You, heart pt.2

You, heart are too irrational
You blank out from facts;
knowing someone's true actions
Right or wrong
Good or bad
You zone in on feelings
What makes you happy in the moment
Sad in the moment
Excited in the moment
Not about the future
You, heart play me a lot
i try to stick to my logical brain
But you, heart always get in the way

Build me a wall

Build me a wall
Straight and symmetric
Perfect to be exact
It hold in feelings
That become too reckless
It can block the strongest
Most powerful feelings
Those feelings are stronger than warriors
Bigger than any beast
Eventually the perfect walls turn weak
The warriors fight back
Bashing the walls in
Colouring her symmetric walls with dirt
They take the wall down
The warriors hurt many
No matter what you do or say
The warriors always come back
To ruin everything
Thanks wall, you tried
Maybe next time you'll survive

Crescent moon eyes

Eyes,
They can tell many disgusting lies
But they are beautiful
No matter what may lie beneath them,
Disguised with the beauty of your crescent moons
i try to make it out alive;
Of your moon like eyes
But i do not succeed
They are too beautiful to resist
i cannot deny
Those crescent moons
They get me every single time

Ice blocks

i feel like i need to cry a lot
But nothing comes out
i guess my eyes are ice blocks

The little things

The little things
So hard to let go
Practically burying me alive
Weighing my whole body down
i don't get why
The little things take such a toll on our lives
Who are they to say;
You won't go out today
Our don't have enough courage to speak at the
assembly
We don't deserve to have little things affect us in big
ways
We should be able to oversee hate
Take on the biggest project with confidence
Not be scared to live our lives the way we like
Will we ever get over the pain of the little thing
i hope one day the little things dissipate

I know the future

We think we know how our futures will go
But in a flash
Everything can be different
Insignificant
Rigorous
We go through life dreaming of what is to come
But what is to come?
When we dream is it reality
Or is it our unconscious minds
Guiding us to where we want to be

Dreams make you believe

Floating in and out of a deep sleep
Dreams pass by our eyes
Like movies on a big screen
They show us things
Weird things and good thing and bad things and new
things
We come alive in our dreams-
Our subconscious is a dangerous thing
It makes us believe
That things have changed
Our hopes have come to life
But when once we wake
The dream vaporizes to memories that can barely be
described
We float back to our conscious minds
Everything we seen is out of reach
Everything is not how we had dreamed
Everything we hoped to change has faded away
Everything we dreamed is gone
Why do dreams make us believe
That things will change
and that life is different
When all they do is make us sad
And have us begging for a difference

No casual dreams

My birthday was the other day
So many people glad to see i was finally fifteen
i want to scream i am not going anywhere
So don't expect me to disappear
Don't be surprised to see me in 20 years
Riding in a private jet
Creating many more edgy limericks
Fifteen does not mean casual dreams

It'll be great

Taking over the world
 Many issues in my mind
Ready to be solved
No time to spare
With you next to me
And them all behind
We'll be great
Better than the rest
Ready to change for the best

Destiny

Sometimes destiny pressures me
To step outside my boundaries
To see what's around me
i don't like to be pressured
But it makes me see the light
i guess that's why we call it destiny
It makes us see what could be
Makes us attempt things
We didn't think were possible
Or at least that's what i think
We all want a destiny
Even if destiny isn't a thing
We need to make ourselves believe
Destiny is a real thing
Yours could be living in Beijing
Or having your own personal hot spring
We can only assume what destiny means
So let's assume
Maybe it'll lead you to something big

Live your life

Why do we let our lives go to waste
Don't just sit and wait
Get up and create
You have one life
One chance
One opportunity
Don't let a bad day;
Bad week
Bad month
Bad year
Take you out
Stay strong
Live your life
Live it 'till there's nothing left to live
Enjoy it
Enjoy it 'till joy is the only thing you need

Knowing

Do we come into life knowing
Knowing who we are supposed to be
Knowing who we are supposed to meet
Knowing why things are meant to be
That's what they say
But who are they?
And how do they know
Who we are supposed to be;
Meet and see

The funny truth

Some days i wake
Ready to take on the day
Confident and beautiful
But some days i don't know what has taken over
Sad and discouraged
No power
No strength
Tomorrow will be a a good day i pray
Get out of bed i tell myself
i just need to get through today

i am women

i feel violated and discriminated
Just because i am women
Does not mean i am more vain and less sane
Does not mean i like dressing up and gossip
Does not mean women have to be a certain size or
weight
Women are bold
Women are beautiful
That is no mistake
From size 0 to size infinity
There's no point in trying to replace
A women's sanguinity

Beautiful

You're beautiful they say
As i walk away i feel like it is the best day
But since when did being called beautiful start making
someone's day?

You are perfect

People always say
You are perfect
But we assume perfect has one definition
But sweetheart
Perfect is universal
Everyone is their own perfect
The height
The hair
The body
The face
The race
All unique and perfect
Perfect to me and perfect to everyone
You'll realize one day no matter how hard you try to deny
You're perfect no matter what you look like

Am i in heaven?

Am i in heaven?
i can't tell just yet because
Smiles are pure
Laughter is to sweet
Winter is to bright
How do these thing not come from heaven
The power of love is too strong
Friends are too kind
Blueberry;
Chocolate
And sparkly green eyes
Cannot be better in heaven
Am i in heaven?
That is a big question
But i will cry 'till i reckon
This has to be heaven
Unless these are all just lucky blessings

What a disappointment

Disappointing parents is the worst feeling in life
They nurture and care for you
Make sure everything is alright
But one day you do something foolish
And your parents lose their patience
"You disappointed me", they say
Your heart drops in dismay
The worst feeling in life has been granted your way
You cry till there's no tears left-
No one to help you through this test
Your support system is gone
Disappointment lies,
You must just hold on
The time will come when they get over it
But the feeling will always sit in your bottomless pit

To my parents

You are filled with all of my questions and all of my
heart. Everything i have i give to You.
Everything i am is because of You.

Earth, right?

This is earth right?
Just making sure i am in the right place
They said it was a disastrous disgrace
Though what they said sounded crazy
Now that i am here i know what they mean
This ugly yet beautiful scene
Full of blood and flood
Yet earth has willpower and many lovely types of flowers
But i don't know if i'll be able to stay
i'll make sure i speak to earth's puppeteer
For now
i will say "May peace touch earth"
There's too many beautiful things for it to be stripped from its worth
Good luck i say to earth
But i am on my way
This is earth, right?
Because i can't stay

Memories aren't real

Memories are associations
Figments of our imaginations
They take a while to come our present thoughts
And though they can be rather unpleasant
We suck it up
And let the memories pile
Someone told me once that memories aren't real
If memories aren't real
How will we know what in life is actual

Ending

To the never ending cycle
Of a teenage brain
So many words
Thoughts
Emotions
i bet you didn't think this young human
Could feel, know and think so many intuitive things
Just like that its the end
Glad you got to witness
What its like in the mind of a teenager

The end

Lightning Source UK Ltd.
Milton Keynes UK
UKHW010614231019
352139UK00001B/41/P

9 781988 762159